H.M. BATEMAN

THE MAN WHO...
and Other Drawings

Edited by John Jensen

A METHUEN HUMOUR CLASSIC

A Methuen Paperback

This collection first published 1975 by
Eyre Methuen Ltd
This paperback edition published 1983 by
Methuen London Ltd
11 New Fetter Lane, London EC4P 4EE

Illustrations © 1975 Estate of H. M. Bateman
Text © 1975 John Jensen

ISBN 0 413 52730 1

Printed and bound in Great Britain by
William Clowes (Beccles) Limited, Beccles and London

Editor's Note

The drawings in this book are not presented in chronological order. Instead they are grouped under general subject headings. In this way, with early and late drawings sitting cheek-by-jowl, it is possible to watch the ingenuity and professionalism with which H. M. Bateman was able to extract from the limits of his material a wide and diverse range of humour.

Acknowledgements

The idea for the book was suggested by Herbert van Thal. I am grateful to Mr and Mrs Dick Willis for their patience and invaluable assistance in its preparation; to Mrs M. Pine and Mrs Brenda Bateman for their enthusiastic encouragement; to Lucy and Henry Willis for their kindness in allowing me to reproduce their unique postcards. Thanks are due to the Proprietors of *Punch* for permission to reproduce copyright material; to Christopher Phillips and the Leicester Galleries for help and generosity in providing some of the prints included in the selection; and to Michael Bateman for permission to use an H. M. Bateman caricature from his collection. I am particularly grateful to my wife, Pat, for her typically practical, professional advice.

Much care has been taken to try to trace the copyright holders of all the drawings in this collection, but if any copyright material has inadvertently been used without due permission or acknowledgement, apologies are offered to those concerned.

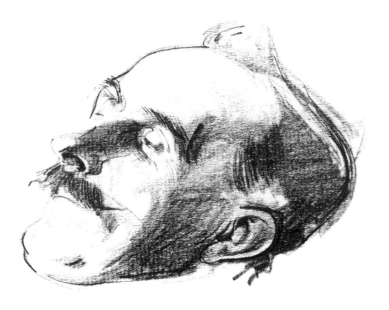

The choice. At the age of twenty-one H. M. Bateman underwent a period of agonizing indecision as he mulled over the opposing aspects of his talent, each one pointing to a different career and a different life. In deciding to 'make people laugh', he remained faithful to a childhood ambition.

Introduction

H. M. Bateman was born in New South Wales, Australia, on 15 February 1887. He died, just a few days short of his eighty-third birthday, in 1970, on the Maltese island of Gozo.

Excluding some extensive travel, the years between were passed in England, mostly in Devon, where he lived quietly, simply and industriously. Shortly after the outbreak of the Second World War a self-imposed semi-retirement reduced the industry and, thereafter, trout fishing with the fly assumed a higher priority.

During the twenties and thirties Bateman's popularity as a cartoonist had reached international proportions, largely on the strength of one versatile idea capable of endless variation. Published as full colour double spreads in the *Tatler*, 'The Man Who . . .' series, while English middle class in outlook and character, struck familiar chords among all types and classes of people everywhere. If the cartoon characters were British, their predicament – their fallibility – was universal, and human fallibility knows no social or political boundaries.

With crisp precision the captions describe the central gaffe, or clanger, of each drawing: 'The Boy Who Breathed on the Glass in the British Museum', 'The Guardsman Who Dropped It', 'The Man Who Lit His Cigar Before the Royal Toast'. Each sets the scene for a gleefully drawn drama of social incompetence, ineptitude, ignorance or folly.

Sometimes oblivious of the turmoil they have produced, at other times crushed with the shame and embarrassment of dawning realization, lonely figures stand surrounded by a dazed, outraged, and incredulous assembly. The joke is as simple as that, but greatness arises from simplicity, and H. M. Bateman was a great humorist.

His stream of inadequates gave the English a vicarious release. With child-like pleasure they were able to participate in a bloodless Roman Circus with Etiquette as the arena. Beneath the Englishman's habitual *sang-froid* (whatever became of *that*, I wonder?) Bateman discerned a thousand volcanoes waiting to erupt and, in his drawings, he allowed them to burst through the surface. Furious characters behave as if they are about to horsewhip an editor; there is about them something of a Latin passion – a vision apoplectic rather than apocalyptic!

A conventional man (though sometimes reluctantly so), H. M. Bateman found

artistic maturity through the chance discovery of a new and unconventional method. To use his own words he 'went mad on paper'. Energies which had been constrained by shyness found their outlet, and the young artist's own inner volcanoes erupted on to paper. Inhibitions and constraint thrown overboard, he began to draw people not as they looked, which was usual, but as they *felt*, which was not. In doing so a new insight and a fresh spirit was introduced into comic art.

The newly found freedom was far from anarchistic. Behind the wildest inspirations lay a sense of artistry based upon a thorough grounding in traditional draughtsmanship. Tuition at the Westminster School of Art and Goldsmith's College was followed by a final polish in the studio of Charles van Havenmaet, who, some years before, had also instructed the illustrator and poster artist, John Hassall. Although he came to bend the rules, Bateman never entirely broke with the basic disciplines of an academic training.

Filled from childhood with an urge 'to make people laugh', Bateman, during his student days, found this unusual and difficult ambition put under severe stress. There were many qualities about his work which suggested a career as a 'serious' artist. In all likelihood his colleagues would have encouraged him in

Influence: Henry Ospovat
Ospovat, a Russian Jew *émigré*, died in the first decade of the century at the age of thirty-one. During his short lifetime a gift for extravagant but accurate caricature earned him a reputation as an 'impish genius'. Fifty years later (in the course of an interview in 1962) Bateman still recalled him as 'Oh – a splendid man!'

this direction, for cartooning was looked upon as a lowly thing. An inner conflict followed. The difficulty – for a highly sensitive young man, the *anguish* – of having to choose from a number of very different skills, techniques, and aptitudes, each with its opposing demands, resulted in a series of acute depressions and, finally, a complete nervous breakdown. Bateman celebrated his twenty-first birthday, miserably, in a sick bed.

The decision was taken during convalescence. It was based not upon aesthetic, artistic, or cultural grounds, but in the knowledge that humour would provide an assured income, whereas art probably would not. Nevertheless, throughout his long life, Bateman occasionally, rather wistfully, hoped to paint a picture which would charm by expressing 'the beauty of earth and sky and water'. Yet in spite of the excellent draughtsmanship, his serious work lacked the inspirational force which gave so much life to his cartoon creations.

During his formative years Bateman's style was shaped by many influences. The illustrations of Arthur Rackham and the caricatures of Max Beerbohm and Henry Ospovat were much admired. The Russian-born Ospovat enjoyed, in his lifetime, a reputation as an 'impish genius'. He died at the tragically early age of thirty-one, in the first decade of this century.

9

The works of the Continental cartoonists were closely followed but Bateman's deepest respect was reserved for the French School and, among many fine talents, above all others, the comic genius of Emmanuel Poiré – *Caran d' Ache* – whose influence was profound and lasting. A Russian-born Frenchman, *Caran d' Ache* was the grandson of one of Napoleon's officers. He died in 1909 at the age of fifty.

It was through the example of *Caran d' Ache* that Bateman found the inspiration which gave him his artistic freedom. His work, dating from this time, 1909, and after, can be divided into two major categories: the early works – the caricatures, and the long series of imaginary Types – which rely for effect upon character

and characterization, and the later drawings which more largely depend upon
situation for their humour. These include the strips-without-words which
Bateman also pioneered in this country.

In spite of their verve, assurance, and apparent spontaneity, the caricatures
were the result of painstaking preparation. Each might be drawn and redrawn,
again and again, in order to capture the elusive nuance or highlight. Given that
the sketches were intended to raise a smile, many of them were imbued with
a sensitivity and subtlety rare in comic drawing. These two qualities were reluctantly but determinedly dismissed from the later, more popular cartoons.
They would have detracted from the joke.

'The Man Who . . .' series can hardly be described as subtle. Nor sensitive. The drawings are bold, and characterization is simple and often deliberately crude. Unlike the earlier caricatures these rooms full of writhing humanity were drawn directly with only the barest of pencil guidelines and without preliminary sketches – apart, that is, from essential reference material noted in the sketchbooks which Bateman habitually carried about with him.

Both early and late drawings were made convincing, no matter how bizarre or exaggerated the context, by a painstaking attention to accuracy of detail. Fashions, automobiles, backgrounds, and the characters themselves are fixed in their time but the jokes, certainly a large number of them, are timeless.

'The Man Who . . .' not only revealed the Englishman beneath the skull, thus providing the artist with his reputation at home, it also hit upon a universal truth, thus assuring him of his place among the immortals. The philosopher Thomas Hobbes (1588–1679) observed 'that the passion of laughter is nothing else but sudden glory, arising from sudden conception of some eminency in ourselves, by comparison with the infirmity of others, or with our own formerly'. The humour and attraction of 'The Man Who . . .' could not be better summed up.

MR. H. M. BATEMAN

requests the honour of a visit from

.... and Friends

at the Private View of his Original

SATIRES & CARICATURES

On Wednesday, July 12th, 1911,

AT THE

BROOK STREET ART GALLERY,

14, BROOK STREET,

NEW BOND STREET, W.

This Card is available until the closing day of the Exhibition,
July 31st, 1911.

10 to 6 daily.   Saturdays 10 to 5.

Caricatures

Lawson Wood
Between the wars Lawson Wood was known as the creator of Gran'pop, a genial, ginger ape much loved in the nursery. Wood was a gifted watercolourist.

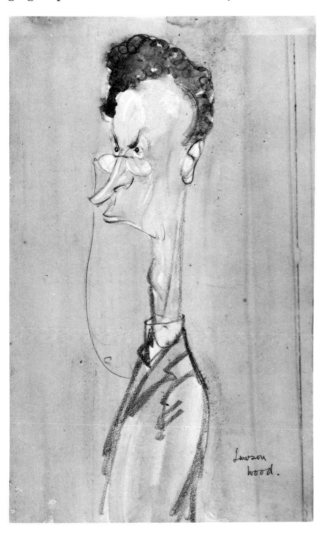

CARICATURES BY H. M. BATEMAN,
No. 13.—Marie Tempest.

Miss Marie Tempest
Actors, actresses and fellow members of the Chelsea Arts Club provided H. M. Bateman with many of his caricature subjects. Although not gifted with profound insight, he was able to twist external features with a wild extravagance. Unusual in a caricaturist, his work reveals more affection than malice. Caricatures formed the bulk of his first one-man show in the West End. *Satires and Caricatures* was shown in 1911 when the artist was twenty-four.

H. M. Bateman's caricatures were drawn mainly from memory. But sometimes, in a complex theatre production perhaps, where a large cast and many costume changes might overwhelm the most retentive mind, quick sketches were a necessity. The full-page theatre caricatures, 'By Our Untamed Artist', which appeared in *The Sketch*, were built from these slightest of notes. The drawing of 'The Pearl Girl' was published in 1913. Among the cast were the young Mr Jack Hulbert and Miss Cicely Courtneidge.

BY OUR UNTAMED ARTIST: "THE PEARL GIRL."

AT THE SHAFTESBURY: CHARACTERS OF THE NEW MUSICAL COMEDY CARICATURED.

The Missed Putt

The Man Who...

The earliest cartoon in which H. M. Bateman drew people not as they looked but as they felt was published in 1909. By no means one of his best drawings, 'The English are a Sporting Nation' nevertheless marked the injection of a new and important spirit into comic art. Three years later the same spirit was more successfully deployed in a wild scene of mass consternation, 'The Missed Putt'. Bateman saw this as the first of 'The Man Who . . .' series.

The English are a Sporting Nation!

17

18

The man who ate his luncheon in the Royal Enclosure

The mother who kissed her son at Lord's

20

The lady who asked for 'Rabbit'

Sable

The woman who spent £10 in a Woolworth store

The shop assistant who lost his temper

The High Priestess

An egg to his tea

24

The grumble-at-the-food-and-everything else person

The diner who addressed the *maître d'hôtel* as 'Garcon'

The guest who called the *foie gras* potted meat

The man who asked for a second helping at a City Company Dinner

29

The maid who was but human

The man who refuses
a drink because he says he
isn't thirsty

The non-drinking host

The girl who ordered a glass of milk at the Café Royal

The Café Royal, in London's Regent Street, was once much more of a café than it is today. It was the haunt of Beardsley, Whistler, and Wilde, of Augustus John, Sickert, Epstein, and Ezra Pound. Among these and other distinguished *habitués* milled a mixture of near-celebrities, hangers-on, poseurs and phonies; the notable and the notorious in worldly abundance. After the evening dinner-rush the less-well-off sophisticates, while no doubt sneering at any young innocent ordering milk, would themselves linger over a sixpenny *mazagran* – iced coffee served in a glass. Black coffee, of course.

Colonels
and Other Ranks

After volunteering for military service during the early days of the First World War,
H. M. Bateman, not a robust man, was briskly returned to civilian life. Throughout the
war and long after, the Services provided material for some of his best cartoons. The
blustering, choleric 'Colonels' were imprisoned for posterity in a collection published
in 1925.

The Colonel's Tie

33

The Commander-in-Chief's trumpeter sounds the 'Dismiss' in error

**The Colonel implores his daughter
to be reasonable**

36   **Two kinds of patience**

The Drum-Major who muffed his catch

DEEDS THAT OUGHT TO WIN THE V.C.
The Sub-Lieutenant takes the Admiral's Queen

One up!

38

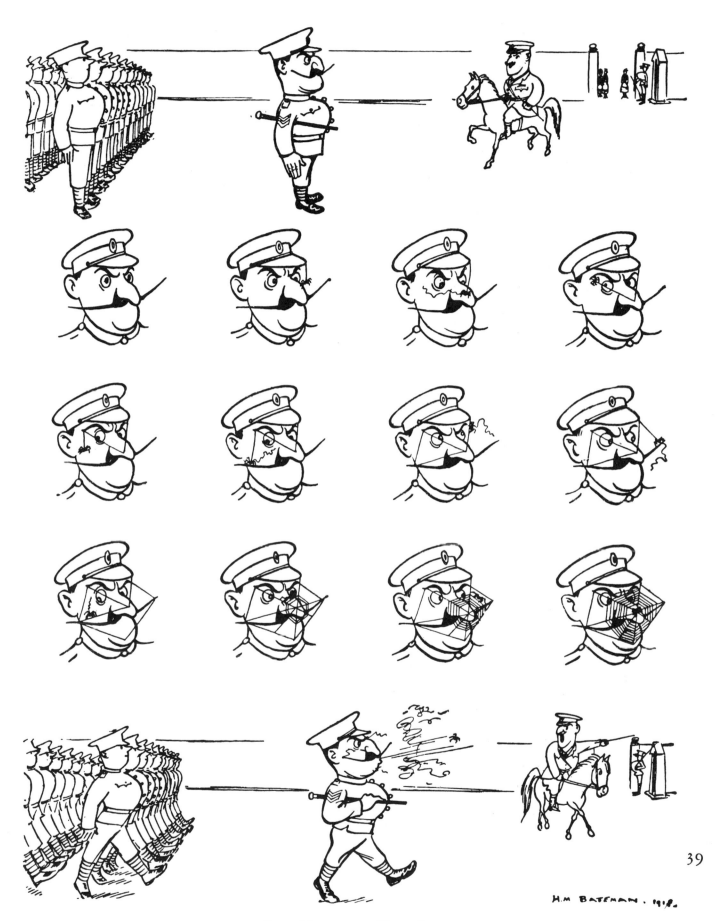

Steadiness on Parade

39

Behind the scenes at Wellington Barracks

41

42

THE EYES OF THE FLEET
or 'Visibility Good'

Hotels and Holidays

The man whose entire outfit of hotel, railroad and steamship
reservations blew overboard

The croupiers who showed signs of emotion

45

**The potter-about-the-hall-
all-day-and-watch-the-funny-people-
come-and-go person**

46

The Wrong Shoes

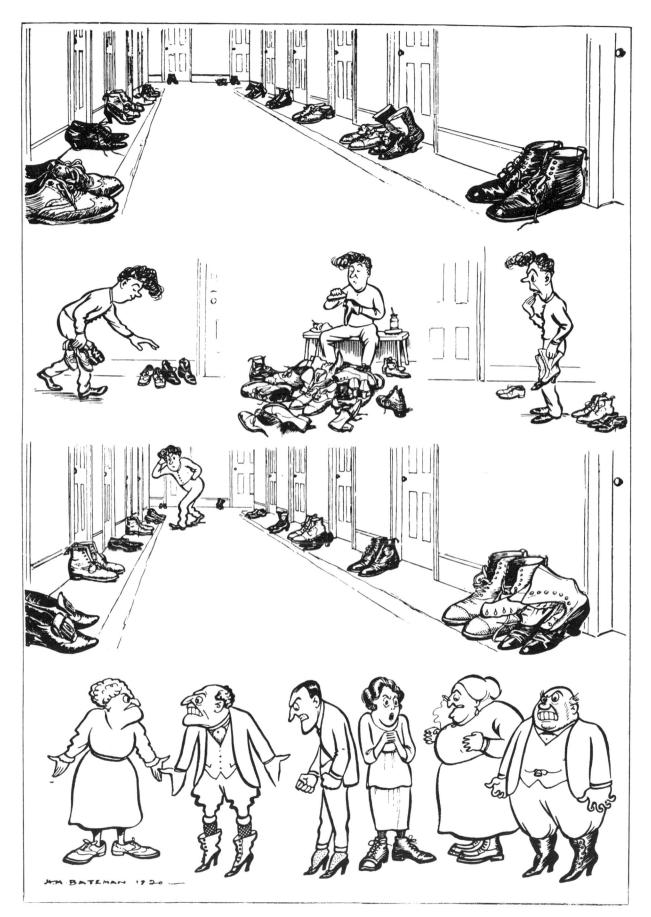

The Boots who forgot to chalk the boots

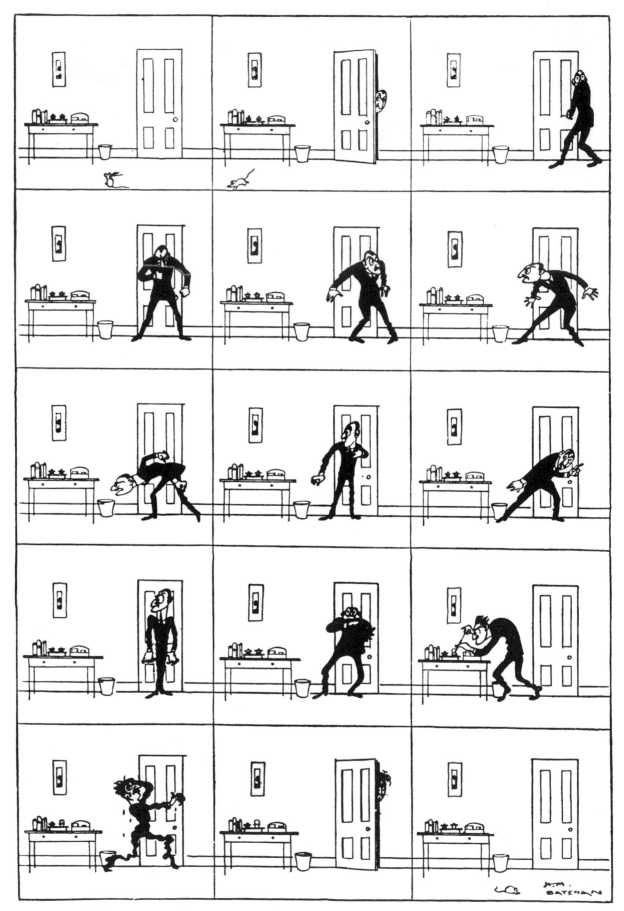

48

The man who filled his fountain pen with the hotel ink

Trials of a Steward

The man who asked for a double scotch in the Grand Pump Room at Bath

H. M. Bateman usually carried a sketchbook about with him. Some of the drawings were highly finished ends-in-themselves. Others were more perfunctory; a means of briefly setting down information for future reference. The transmogrification of un-adorned pencilled notes into a comic masterpiece can be seen in these sketches for one of his most famous cartoons, 'The man who asked for a double scotch in the Grand Pump Room at Bath'. The drawing now belongs to the Corporation of Bath. Another Bateman classic, 'The Boy Who Breathed on the Glass in the British Museum', resides, appropriately, in the British Museum.

This is how the Jacksons felt and looked on getting back from a fortnight's stay at Slopton-on-Sea, during which time it rained without a break.

And this is how they looked and felt later, on hearing from the Robinsons that they had gone down to Slopton-on-Sea on the same day the Jacksons returned, and had since been enjoying unbroken fine weather!

Sport

Incroyable

The Drive

In his sketchbooks H. M. Bateman often noted down cartoon ideas and captions, as they occurred to him, for future use. Sketches for 'The Drive' were made around 1912. The drawing was completed and published in 1932.

The new word in golf

56

Shy

57

H.M. BATEMAN.

58

The Crisis : Tattenham Corner

The Winner : Ascot

59

Intimidation

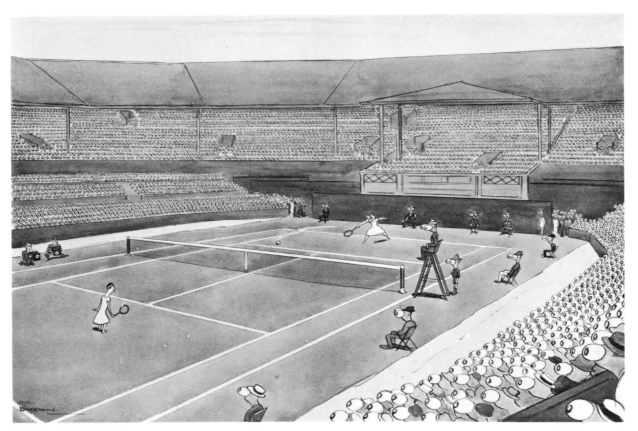

The Débutante

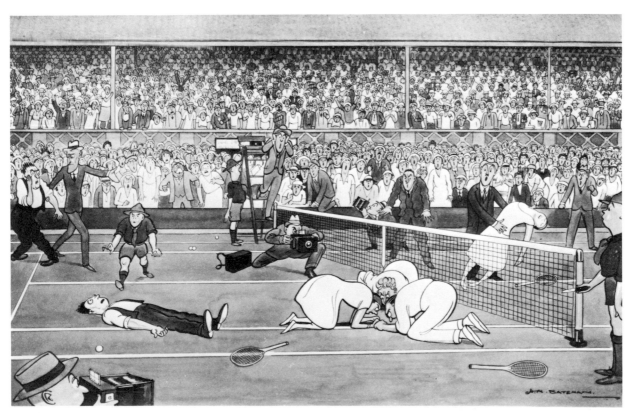

Discovery of a dandelion on the Centre Court at Wimbledon

61

A Cowes Nightmare – The Unwelcome Guest

63

THE OLD MOUNTAINEERS
Suggestion for the Alpine Club

Vice Versa

A version of 'Vice Versa' is to be found in one of the 1912–13 sketchbooks. Completed in 1959, the drawing is published here for the first time, some sixty years after it was first conceived.

The Unexpected Call

Mr Smith, in the course of conversation produces a beautiful RUMOUR taking the form, as it leaves him, of a perfect sphere –

– which is caught up by Brown, who at once transforms it into a square –

– passing on to Tomkins, whom it leaves in the shape of an unknown geometrical problem, for –

– Watson, who shrinks it to a little worm-like thing.

Mrs Robinson, however, expands it, but in the nature of a star, before handing on to –

Jackson, who at once shatters it into a million fragments while –

– passing it to Baxter, who restores it to the original sphere, though in three separate portions, which are dealt –

– with by Lewis, after which it has no definite form, being rather that of a cloud of vapour.

In due course it comes back to Mr Smith, who quite fails to recognize it as as his own creation.

The Adventures of a Rumour

The fashions have changed but in their essentials many of H. M. Bateman's subjects remain timeless. Others have gained an unexpected topicality. The drawings which follow, in their varying ways and in varying degrees, reflect much that is familiar in our world today, even though they were drawn, many of them, more than half a century ago.

They call it 'Fame'

The girl who thought she would like a
snapshot of the Prince

Engaged!

The Cautious Life

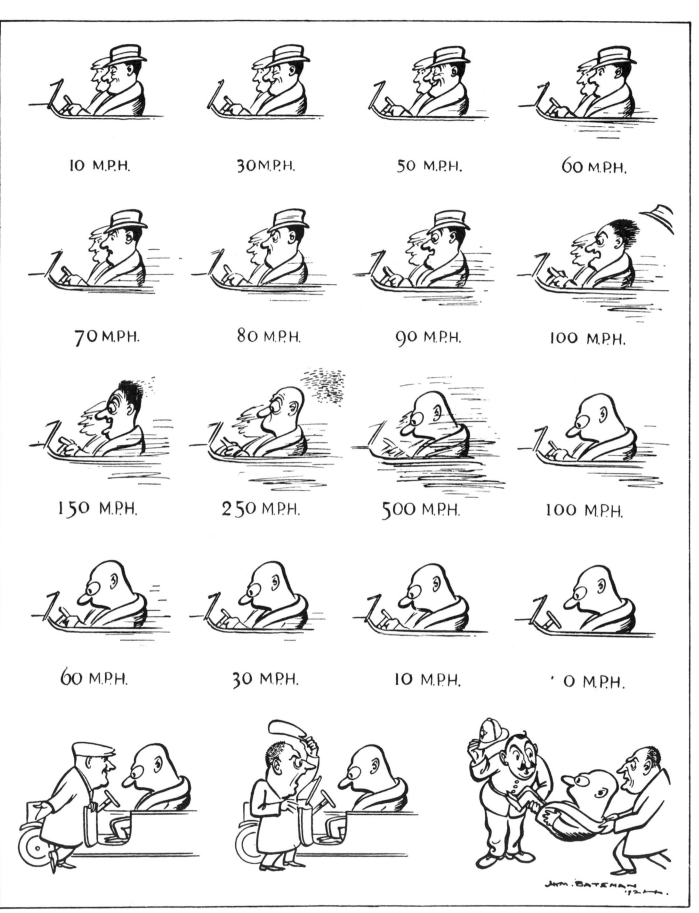

The man who watches the speedometer

Inducing the Chairman to face the shareholders

The Millionaire

The Socialist

Coronas

Some do it by the raising
of an eyebrow,

Some by a slight inclination
of the head,

Some with a wink,

Some by adjusting their tie,

Some by elevating the
catalogue –

or a forefinger,

Some by the removal of
their spectacles,

Another by replacing them,

But the heathen – he does
it by word of mouth.

75

The Art of Bidding

The Late Arrivals

76

**The couple who caught
their last train**

The Sexless Play

Man and Wife

'Man and Wife' was drawn in 1911. Looking back half a century later, H. M. Bateman wrote, 'So far as I am able to judge my own work it is one of my best of that period and one I liked'.

79

The man who bought tickets for the wrong night

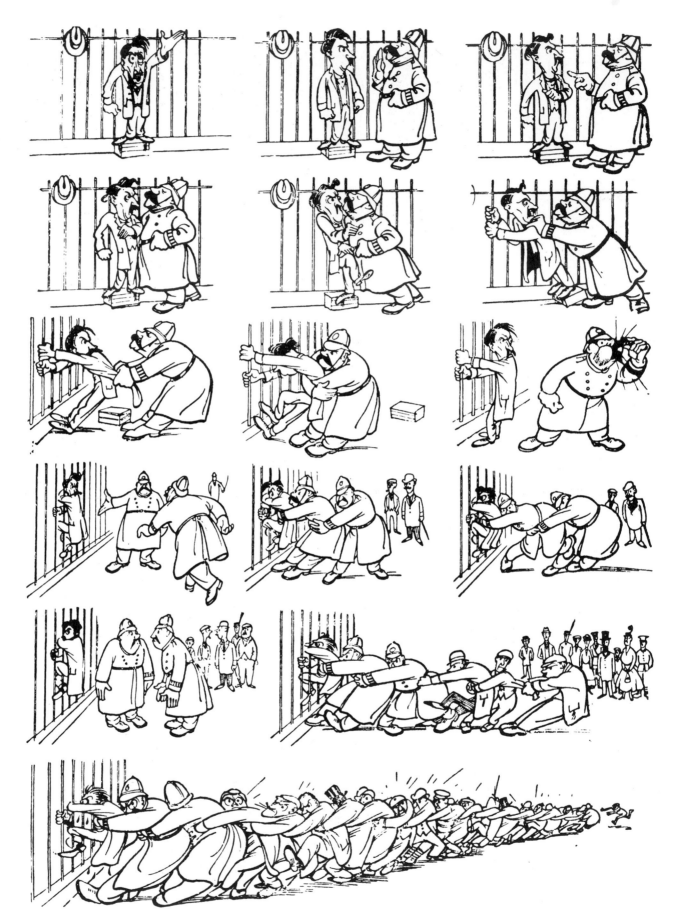

80

'Prisoner, when arrested, clung to the railings'

81

The False Income-Tax Return – and its rectification

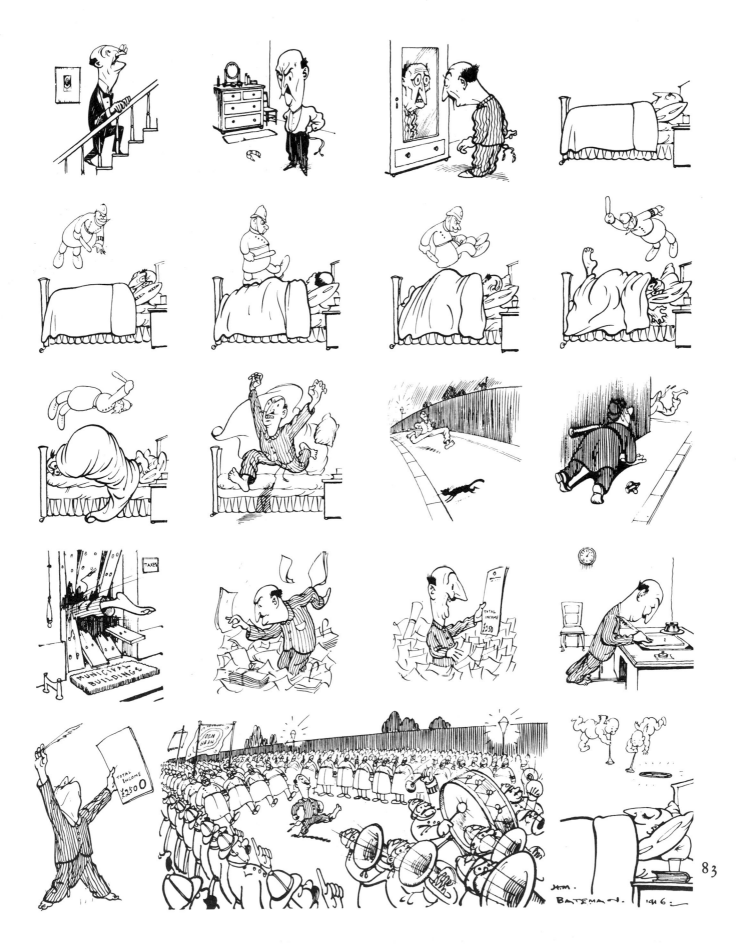

83

THE CAR COST THREE THOUSAND POUNDS – TO SAY NOTHING OF ITS UPKEEP – AND HER COAT SEVEN HUNDRED AND FIFTY GUINEAS. YET SHE EMPLOYS THEM TO MOTOR SOME FORTY ODD MILES —

H.M. BATEMAN.

INTO TOWN IN ORDER TO TAKE PART IN A STRUGGLE TO SECURE THE ADVANTAGE OF A SPECIAL REDUCTION OF THREE HALFPENCE PER YARD ON SOME CRETONNE SHE NEEDS.

Speaking recently before a distinguished Society an architect named a village which, to his surprise, although close to its outskirts, did not seem to be known to the people of the City.

Fortunately the matter was reported in the Press – and the error repaired.

85

Aunty's Ecstasy

CHRISTMAS!

How some celebrate it . . .

. . . and others

87

The Two Uncles

A heart-to-heart talk

The Bachelor

H. M. Bateman all by Himself

A conformist aware of the constraints of conformity, H. M. Bateman sometimes complained of feeling 'caged in'. The cartoon opposite suggests he was also aware of the obverse of *that* coin – that those who are not caged in are invariably caged out!

Mirabile Dictu
(Wonderful to Tell : Virgil)

Firenze - Cappelle Medicee - Monumento a Giuliano de' Medici
(Michelangiolo).

94

'FALCON HOTEL'
BROMYARD.

Having Wonderful Time...

H. M. Bateman did not marry until he was nearly forty. Although he came late to grand-parenthood he enjoyed his young grandchildren enormously and, in old-age, delighted in delighting them by sending postcards to which he had added a small, apposite, pictorial libel of himself. The accompanying texts were usually as relaxed and quietly amusing as the drawings.

'There – see what travel does for you! Knocks the
corners off and makes you a different person. Of course
the bottom may drop out of it sometime.'

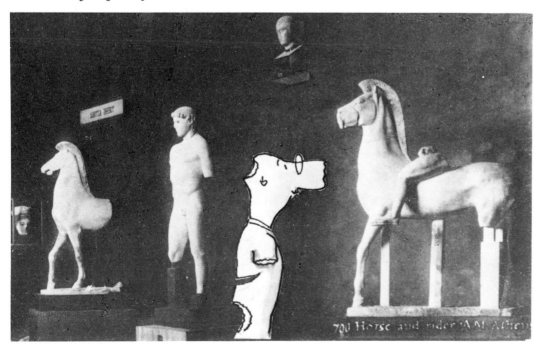

95

Portrait of the Editor
by H. M. Bateman

Born in 1930, the cartoonist son of a cartoonist father, John Jensen (the name is adopted) is a fourth-generation Australian of Scottish descent. Currently the political cartoonist of the London *Sunday Telegraph*, social cartoonist of *The Spectator* and theatre caricaturist of the *Tatler*, his work, since his arrival in Britain in 1949, has appeared in many national and international magazines, including *Punch*, and he has illustrated more than thirty books. A sometime Secretary of the British Cartoonists' Association, Mr Jensen was on the organizing committee of the cartoon exhibition, *Drawn and Quartered*, held at the National Portrait Gallery in 1970. He is now compiling a life of the late, Australian, Radical cartoonist, Will Dyson. His familiarity with the work of H. M. Bateman dates back to early childhood – his nursery books were cartoon collections given to him by his father. Married with two children, recreations include music when his two boys permit, and walking when they do not.